CROWS

The stars reside
in a cold, cold place
of infinite darkness
but the dark within
is the cold itself
hand packed
with four sides and two ends—
flavor of failure and desire
fed to the stars
with the moon's
flat white spoon
from bowls of hours.

Acknowledgments

"The Navigator of Light," "The Vacation," "Fireflies," and "Channings (by the side of the river)." Various issues of *The Tufts Review*.

"Minding the Absence," "Lepidoptera," and "Mickle Street." *White Hours*, PeKa Boo Press, 1981.

"Ash," "Front Yard Maple," "Sparrows," and "Rest." *Leaves*, PeKa Boo Press, 1983.

"Ice Irises," "Just like That," and "January Morning." *Ice Irises*. PeKa Boo Press, 1984.

"Day Lily," "Blue Chicory," "The Kingdom of Sand," "Beach Grass," and "Wildflowers." *Wildflowers*, PeKaBoo Press, 1984.

"Wildflowers." *Woods Hole Passage*.

"Woods Hole Passage." *Cape Cod Life*.

"Mosquito Dance." *The Torch*.

"The Wasp," "Freeing the Potatoes," "Untitled Morning Song," and "The Bird." *Defining a Plane*, poems by Eric Edwards, Judith Richardson and James Morgan, Harlequin Ink, 1991.

"The Big E." *Cimarron Review*.

"Digging a Hole in The Earth," "Freeing the Potatoes," "Rest," and "The Dog." Various issues of *The Onset Review*.

"I, Terrorist." Correspondence, *Thought & Action*.

"Returning to a Place" and "Stone Hunters." *Sonoma Mandala*.

ONE BIRD BOOKS
AVAILABLE AT AMAZON.COM
Door by Mary Kane
The Ant and the Map by Judith Benét Richardson
Harlequin's Guitar: A Fable in 67 Improvisations by Jim Morgan
Little Hours: A Novel by Lil Copan
Luminous: a forty-four day exchange while wandering *The Tibetan Book of the Dead* by Mary Kane and Mark Bilokur
Black Apple: Collected Prose Poems 1975-2022 by Eric H. Edwards
In the Book I'm Reading by Mary Kane

Crows

POEMS

Jim Morgan

One Bird Books • Hatchville, Mass.

Copyright ©2023 Jim Morgan
All rights reserved.

Editor: Mary Kane
Design and layout: Jim Morgan
Art: Mark Bilokur
Cover design: Jim Morgan

Special thanks to my wife, Deb,
to Mary Kane, and to Eric H.
Edwards and Judith Benét Richardson,

ONE BIRD BOOKS
35 Brush Hill Road
Hatchville, MA 02536
www.onebirdbooks.com
onebirdbooks@gmail.com

ISBN-13: 978-1-7339200-4-9

Contents

Minding the Absence	1
The Navigator of Light	2
The Vacation	3
Fireflies	4
Channings (by the side of the river)	5
Wood Lily	7
Mickle Street	8
Front Yard Maple	9
Sparrows	10
Just Like That	11
Ice Irises	12
January Morning	13
Herons	14
Ash	15
Rest	16
Day Lily	17
Blue Chicory	18
The Kingdom of Sand	19
Beach Grass	20
Wildflowers	21
Woods Hole Passage	22
Fish Father	23
Winter	25
Spring	26
Iris	27
The Wasp	28
Freeing the Potatoes	29
Untitled Morning Song	31
The Bird	33
After the Hurricane	34
Summer Tree	35
At the Lahey Clinic	37
The Poet's House	38
Winter Stone	40
Big E	41

Digging a Hole in the Earth	43
Firm But Sensible Eating	44
Harlequin Off the Highway	45
Blue Jay Feather	47
Broken Glass	48
Falmouth, Early Morning	50
Forsythia and Lilac	51
Concord Afternoon	52
Another Poem About Stones	53
Leaf, Moon, Word	55
Bird House	56
On a Photograph of Walt Whitman	58
The sea has run away tonight,	59
The Man Who Fell in Love with the Moon	60
Tree Time	61
Leaving This	62
The Story of Falling	63
Starling in a Cedar Tree	64
Ode to the Catbird	65
Leda and the Swan	67
On the Infidelity of Birds	68
At Forty-four	71
Fragment on Tree and Leaf	72
Returning to a Place	73
Arguing with Bakhtin in the Employment and Training Office in Wareham, Mass.	74
Hands	77
A Drunken Moth	78
The Fish in the Bays Grow Fatter	79
Stone, Shell, Crab	80
Who Knows	81
So We Sit	82
Sleep	83
The Body of Rain	84
Low Windows	85
At the Boston Ballet	86
Cobalt Blue Rock	87

What's at Hand	88
Inarticulate Hands	89
Living by Words Alone	90
Poem Without Words	91
Tableau Vivant	92
Coyote Visit	93
November Night	94
On the Poems of Frederico Garcia Lorca	95
Cemetery	96
Shaken by a Dream	97
Snake Crossing	98
The Dog	99
Virgin Mary Reported in Market	100
Vow	103
Confession	104
The Journey of the Hero at the End of the Twentieth Century or: Ted Meets Sylvia in Hell	105
Dream of the Ghost Without Hunger	107
Ode to the Crossword Puzzle	108
Elixir	109
Poem for the New Millennium	110
Crow(s)	111

VIII

FOR EARTH
and all who live here:
live long and prosper

x

Minding the Absence

Birds biting wind
leap in a crowd
south toward cedars.

Wintering, they step
down to low branches,
stuff feathers with cold air
and stand northward
into snow,
minding absent things.

A few die,
aging with stones
under evergreen limbs
until wet March
takes their eyes.

Those who survive,
swollen with spring song,
survive weather by becoming
their own weather,

uncaring and unkind
as they climb
the ladder of trees.

The Navigator of Light

When you emerge
from winter whiteness
a brilliant memory,
do you remember
the weariness of your many feet,
the ponderous inching
over a leaf's eternity,

still-wet wings
fanning the sun
with earth's assurances,
a taste of mud, perhaps,
in your mouth,
an insect's scrutiny of light
and night celebrations?

Flittering flier
rowing your wings,
bicycler spilled by wind,
syllable of colors
searching for nectar,
a partner,
and your eggs' designated host,
where do you buy your paint,
self-made bird
risen from your ashes

only to vanish in a sea of daylight
amid the applause of leaves
from which you come,
trailing summer's four silk scarves.

The Vacation

The moon unsheathes the hills.
Decaying birch lingers in the air.
Every path leads to water
pulling a snagged shore
to the lake of dreams.

Each leaf whispers your name
where none know you.
No fear goes untouched;
even those not yours
have, for now, become so,
taking the shapes of trees and animals,
old lovers, friends, acquaintances.

Examine the details:
a childhood friend appearing
in the wrong city; someone
who deserted you saying,
I loved you too well;
one who leaped from a bridge
winters ago picked up now
by headlights on the edge of your road,
thumbing a ride, knowing
one day you'll stop the car
and open the door.

Fireflies

I'm in love with a woman
who fades from my hands
like smoke from trees,
like the sun dropping into fields
as fireflies, tiny
soft stars skittering across the yard,
beckoning silent males.

Perhaps this is why she has the power
to coax the moon from shadows
and draw me like the sea.

But I cannot stop her from becoming a ghost
who vanishes lying next to me in bed
any more than the sea grasps the moon.
I cannot tear her from darkness.

The sea and I wait for our lovers
to return from their silences,
for the moon to wax round as a cat's face,
for the sun to leap from earth,
leaving it to heave with wind and rain.

I know she'll find me
carrying some crazy lantern
I can't see.

CHANNINGS (BY THE SIDE OF THE RIVER)

Though we slept together as children,
one young and one middle-aged,
I don't know, even now,
years beyond the difficult fear
of the simple middle-age world you inhabit,
if I could sleep beside you,
listening to Sadie's rhythmic, sonorous
waves materialize from their lonely past.

I haven't forgotten.
You're Essie's child, not Sadie's,
but these images won't leave one another alone,
coupled like coal cars
dragging their slack weight,
picking a way among mountains
with black loads of the once living.

I want you to know I'm ashamed of that fear
of your weakness, your innocence
undefinable as the darkness settling
across these hilly fields. Yet even
my shame is harmless
to you, protected by some silent blessing
upon those held innocent
against all will.

Without such blessing,
I cannot tell you except here
where it will never reach one
who never learned to read.

Mother knew
you're the happiest of us,
any worries milked from your head:
a soft, pink teat Henry grappled
like a cow udder as you emerged

from the liquid, red, swollen dawn
into your new world.

Even you knew not to take those chances
and died, there and then.

Henry, familiar with calving and,
probably, scared shitless,
fathered you twice,
a second coming of breath
your hands clenched instinctively
as the current pushed you back
toward the river of life.

All these years later I lie in bed
amid the traffic's swirl and unforgiving past
while you sit on the porch
eight hundred miles away,
an old, simple man watching stars
fly out of the night sky
and collect along a hill across the river.

In daylight, the Little Kanawha resembles coffee
spilled by lovers escaping your world,
you who have never known the willowy length
of woman, nor, as far as I know,
ever wanted to,
born not from a mother
but from a father's will.

Wood Lily

You saw on the woods' edge
one of the unspoken,
silent beyond adoration
and breathless as words.

The wood lily so claimed the earth
scarlet with its petals
that bringing it home
you were brushed with sadness.

Had you forgotten
what desires to be taken
endlessly returns?

MICKLE STREET

Love is like hair:
the older you become the less you have
and what's left turns white with despair.

Front Yard Maple

In October,
the maple tree turns
yellow and red as the sun

and then empty
as a heart
full of bones,

not the first bare tree
to feign perfectly
and live.

Sparrows

On the triptych window
autumn hellfire –
from the holy tabernacle of cold burning leaves
sparrows stare frightened
of me staring out.

If only I hadn't seen them
undoing their wings.

They do not move,
don't even shriek.
I'm scarier than a cat,
scarier than the leaves' red desertions.

Just Like That

A bird flies out of the sky
into someone else's lifetime.
Not yours.

Just like that.

Hail fell,
bounced,
starring the ground
he ran into
without a sound
from the heart.

Just like that.

We buried him between potato farms.
No clouds.
An autumn field dying with sunlight
where birds fly
a lifetime.

Just like that.

Ice Irises

Ice irises still
cling this morning,
white sprays bent
with heaviness across
the windowpanes.

On the road to work
the sun lifts above the trees,
scrub pines and oaks whose upheld hands,
faintly red where the last leaves fell,
feel the winter light begin to thaw
and run off toward the sea

while ice irises
grow cold as moonlight.

January Morning

The bird singing
from the hobbled oak
beyond the window

was as loud in snow silence
as the rain slick oaks
last fall, uproarious with grackles

though alone and vanished
before I could see
whose bird she was.

Herons

Four herons the color of dried wood
stood in the tidal river, silent as statues of saints.

We drove across the bridge three times and then, by stopping,
frightened them into lifting long, slow wings,

flying like broken water upriver into winter reeds,
leaving the silence to heal.

Ash

Full-leafed with flat palms
the green ash
sways

bends and bows — swept,
battered, rain slick —
and comes back
near upright.

Too often this has happened
so close to the sea
for the young ash
to stand straight again,
though perfect as the things that are.

Rest

Let my ankles rest,
my knees unbend,
thighs and hands,
my lips,
my eyes.
Let my tongue lie
still as a winter snake,
my heart asleep
in a field of red snow.

Yes, you are right and my friend
for telling me.
I no longer dream otherwise.

Tonight the trees
stand like horses
breathing softly
to themselves.
We are so quiet
silence loses hold
over our bodies,
leaving us like these branches.

One day we will wake
to each other
or whatever has entered
among us
while silence lay dumb
and snow fell.

Day Lily

Past day lily
and the green sunsets of leaves,
over planks crossing salt streams
and fiddler crabs scurrying
with their bones to the sea,
a bruised white shell
like a throat lies on the beach.

What would the dead say?

The surprised sadness of leaving off
an afternoon walk in the sun,
the ancient prayers of trees,
and whatever it means
to be born and fall in love
as often as the leaves themselves
and as fatally strong,
words left like sand
to make up the world
they spoke of so often,
among the wild day lily roots.

Blue Chicory

On a bed of stone
where skunks sniff
on the way somewhere,

pressed with prayer,
beneath trees, small
circles of flower,

dog-eared blue chicory.
Ravished to the ground,
they never climb

more than a few feet
under the weight
of outstretched arms.

The blue hands
taste bitter
as earth.

The Kingdom of Sand

I saw you at the ocean
carrying a beach chair.
You wore an old fashioned bathing suit
and once, sadly, called to me.

You walked on.
It was July.
The tide was in
and the sun like hard rain.

You walked to your mother's house,
where we first met,
leaving me the kingdom of sand
and everything that lives in the sea.

I had so much to say
nightmares blistered my tongue.

Was it sadness,
those frail, pink flowers growing
from the corners of your mouth?

After you passed into the sun
all the wild sea roses
turned to dragons
with white teeth
snapping the air.

Beach Grass

Leaf, stem,
the roots' mouthful of sand
but flowerless, flowerless,
no bell or bee to bless
with holy dust.
Who carries the stars
beyond your grasp?

The sun pares
sand from your feet,
leaving each step untied
to fall back into the sea.

What becomes of your green heart?

A wild, swayed desire,
a pain made visible like fish
beneath the clear morality of motion?

Wildflowers

Do not ask much of them.

They are only wildflowers
spread along the edges of sunlight
and men.

They do not last
but flourish and die,
returning on the wind's long hands.

Illuminations,
not texts,
nothing in themselves
and quiet as stars

swaying between
the light we cannot see
and the darkness we can.

Woods Hole Passage

They say the surest way to pass through
is to avoid Broadway and come in
straight for the steamship dock
until you pick up can no. 1
across from red nun no. 2
during the four minutes of slack water
when the currents, losing sight of the moon,
run in no direction
and lay down on Middle Ledge to sleep.

Here the lost and confused come to rest,
aground on the bottom of daylight
that isn't on any map on any placemat
in any fried fish take out
and even Peter couldn't talk his way through
except by walking off the bridge in Newport
carrying every word he possessed,
knowing we would burn that fat corpse
and drop the ashes where blue fish would find them
and carry them through whichever way
they happened to be traveling at the time.

Fish Father

Fish father,
eyed shadow hovering in shallow water,
fin flailing a sandy bed
fanned for a fish mother
to drop her clear vowels
as you pass over,
a silent hand trailing
your strong rain.

I thought you were mistaken,
holding July vigil for the unborn dead,
small mouthed
bass father
color of wet stones.

I thought you the fish mother
as I fed you silvered bait minnows,
spoons flashing in your thick-lipped mouth.

I fished before
and fished after
but did not fish for you,
fish father,

driven to the water's edge,
biting my heels
when I step too close,
your two gold-leaf eyes
focused on their separate worlds,
before and after fish,
unclosing,
you who lie hidden by water:
hovering fish father
revealed.

How many fish mothers
did you lure to your sandy bowl
to pierce their vowels with your white stream?

For I found you sweeping the waters
for your black progeny,
spilled celery seed
beyond the rock tip
of everywhere but water
and you
fine-boned,
white-fleshed, faithful.

The fish mothers all vanish
into the fish-dark depths
to their home among the stones
and cold, cold waters,
leaving you forgotten and alone
to tend the black seed
blossoming within your sun-splintered bowl.

Winter

The sand-colored land breaks
into utterance, flags and fails.

Still winter, still winter, the broken weeds
centered in the heart thrown wildly apart,

flowers turned inward like the flames
extinguished from candles, or wine

the pale color of apple eaten
wherever winter begins or ends,

where memory and leaf fall to the delirium
of air, sharpening themselves to knives:

the cut darkness bleeds starlight,
wind gathers the heart's white seeds.

Spring

For whom do angels open and dance
along thin forsythia branches?

The Iris

The iris that is not a rose
without thorns,
without a taste for blood,
without scent folded
within a radiant center.

Not that red flower
but indigo
with a spotted, yellow throat.

It would hold bees on its tongue
if it spoke their languages.

It would speak syllables of wind
and lines of rain,
burn at night on a green stem
to illumine the pathways of snails and toads
wandering among grass blades,
beyond the trees' fingertips,

the earth packed against its skin,
lying cold as apples
among leaves and snow
until awakened once more.

The Wasp

Having shaken the frail waters
from its wings and tried
thin red legs like runners on old sleds,
the wasp rubbed daylight in its eyes, heaved itself up on the glass
and set off across the clear, luminous world,
the hard, difficult plane of existence
inexplicable with promise
and the worshipful trees beyond
that it will never reach,
having mistakenly entered on the wrong side of an invisible and illusory world
it will measure and misunderstand.

So I killed it.

Freeing the Potatoes

Because I no longer
loved them
I took those that lay

long forgotten,
soft, wrinkled, old
brown ones

worshipping beneath the chalk-white
spires,
their kingdoms

uprooted,
restless ones
impatient

to enter the endless
hallways
of starches.

I flung each
through the trees'
raised arms,

releasing each wingless
from the ground's
come. I have flung

brown-edged limes,
blue powdered breads,
glassy cucumbers,

desiccated oranges,
whitened grapefruit,
soft onions.

All have answered,
angel-eyed,
obedient

to that which loves them
more than I
and takes them in its mouth

home to the good
earth,
and eats them.

Untitled Morning Song

At 4:30 a.m. I ask
the dark, Whose blood isn't all wrong?

From the oak tree just beyond the window
a bird falls softly into morning song.
On the highway,
stray automobiles crisscross the dying night with the white noise
of hoarse breaths.

Lying inside my own darkness
I cannot identify the solitary song,
a jumble of warbles, whistles and chatter
slowly growing insistent.

Insistent upon what?

In a break in the distant traffic
I hear other birds joining in
from other trees and bushes.
I hear what Beethoven silently listened to
in the fourth movement of the last symphony.

Catbird? No,
mockingbird of course,
singing ever more loudly in the oak tree,
singing ever longer lines of notes beyond the window.

A ripe seed falls
to the ground
and stops.

Whatever blood disturbance
felled the mockingbird into song
is satisfied,
or overpowered.

A shadow lifts from the grey leaves
expecting each day
yet no less astonished by light
than I am.

The Bird

On the road
a broken-winged bird
spins, a feathered compass on its good foot.

Rosa rugosas bloom whitely.
Wild grape tendrils upward.
The sea washes its stones.
Between strokes, insects run over sand
as grasses wind dance.
The sea is the green of white wine bottles.
Further down, a pair of abandoned shoes toes the waterline,
waiting.

Which is worse,
sudden death
or waiting helplessly to be eaten?

The bird doesn't speak,
tells me nothing of its life story,
why it deserves to live,
how it only wanted a few crumbs,
which way it may wish to die.

Frightened by cars passing carefully on both sides,
it eyes me warily.

I walk on,
toward the sea the green of wine bottles,
but the sea is too far,
and I return:

the bird is there,
the bird is not there;

the bird is gone,
the bird is not gone.

After the Hurricane

an ocean storm
          leaves wither
     lilac blooms in autumn

Summer Tree

We sat under a summer tree.
She said, *If you're so innocent,*
how come you fall like ripe fruit?
So I gave her references,
the names of women
I loved and once loved me.

Then we sat under the summer tree
and she said, *One remembers you like a son,*
one that you fought like children.
One recalls your hands.
One said you weren't ambitious
and she lost respect for you sleeping around.
One said not being handsome
provided security but you
didn't appreciate winter.
One wanted a father
and found one.
One was stalked by death
and wanted out.
Most have married and
become too smart to answer.
No one says you were too kind.

So we sat under the summer tree
and she said, *How come no one hates you,*
wants to walk through your guts like dead leaves,
scatter your dry, flame-red heart to the winds?

We sat under the summer tree and she said,
Love is meaningless without hate
and I'm leaving for someone strong enough for both.
I said, You only know the half of it.
I'm no angel.
Hate the truth, not me.

She said, *This is the truth.*
Love isn't worth loving.

She left the summer tree.
Summer wavered in the dry, empty heat of memory,
the humidity of desire.

At the Lahey Clinic

On the stone ledge outside the cafeteria
the wind picks at feathers
on a dead pigeon
molting for the last time,
carries off gray ash
from the grate of bones.

In the corner
another sits on a low nest,
steel blue patched with white,
black wings swept back into tuxedo tails.

The chairs sleep
in the early morning.
The pigeon and I
watch air clarify with light

until she is summoned from beyond
and disappears into yellow trees,
leaving two white eggs.

The dead pigeon quietly smolders.
The other returns bearing a small stick,
having found what was missing.

The Poet's House

        A blue door in a white wall,
the house, also white, plain, rectangular.
                Lavender flowers bloom in the yard.
                To the right, a plum tree.

      Unimmortalized,
            second generation,
the plum tree recalls what is lost,
but the house remains, if not beautiful,
            reluctantly true:
                    two kitchens and wine cellar,
                    couch by the front window,
                    a bedroom, small table, two chairs.

One sees the poet
        stooping to clean the lint from between his
                toes
      before ascending
            the high-minded, narrow bed,
                alone
      coughing blood.

      Even the rooms disbelieve
in the solitudes of rhyme, solicitudes of meter,
            yet some poetry remains, discarded, left behind
              where a dusk-dim
                    nightingale
      drew the poet half in love with death
within the shadowy plum.

        In the yard below,
            he wrote the truth faithfully
      as imagination allowed him
          to hear it

                    sung
            among dry plum leaves,
then grew ill
            and travelled south on his way
      somewhere
                  to die.

Winter Stone
For Eric Edwards

Some things love a stone:
beets, tea, peanuts, spinach, chocolate, tofu.

My friend twisted as a root
writhes in the religious ecstasies of Quakers
and howls an ancient hymn
after swallowing the new moon
and carrying it around in his kidney.

Snow swept to the sea and thrown at the stars,
I spend the afternoon sharpening pencils.

Big E

I rise at 5 leave the house by 6 and drive in morning darkness to the Burger King on Rte. 132 which I expect on a Saturday in February to be deserted without summer tourists but isn't the parking lot full of SUVs maneuvering like grey whales on wheels for the few empty spaces people with suitcases boarding buses for Logan and a flight somewhere but I wait with a group of mostly middle-age men for a charter trip to the Big E model railroad show in Springfield the trip taking three hours during which Columbia falls from the sky as I talk to the psychologist in the next seat who tells me men are interested in trains because locomotives are like big pricks I thank Dr. Freud and ask if we project onto them our need for power a compensation for aging for what we lost in childhood and never found mentioning my own father's absence perhaps creating a lifelong desire and my friend says all fathers were absent then and says again trains are like big pricks and laughs until we arrive and wander with thousands of men and women adults and children the elderly and handicapped all drifting by hundreds of tables covered mostly with electric trains of all sizes some toys and some not some plain and some intricate as watches some simple and some with computer systems squeezed into steam engines electrics and diesels painted in art deco styles Santa Fe War Bonnet and New York Central lightning stripe Pennsylvania Brunswick green Western Pacific silver and orange Boston and Maine maroon and yellow Union Pacific yellow and green Texas Special red Southern Pacific orange Canadian Pacific gray maroon and yellow Southern green and gold B&O blue the colors repeating on cabooses and rolling stock and boxcars and tank cars and gondolas and crane cars reefers and hoppers milk cars and flat cars auto carriers and stock cars on defunct railroads still operating on layouts run by club members interspersed with engineer hats and t-shirts lanterns and timetables fare boxes and conductor caps train books and videos eating a hot dog a pretzel and drinking two bottles of water until we return at dusk amid snow

descending to the bus for the ride home only a few of us
having heard the morning's catastrophe I carrying a map
mounted on cardboard of the Pennsylvania Railroad with the
blue track running from Hudson to Akron behind the house
I grew up in we got used to the windows rattling as the trains
rolled past in the night crawling beneath the cars on the
siding the pennies we placed on the rails flattened and a
photograph I will give to my father on his birthday in honor
of his father a West Virginia farmer who in the winters
worked as a boilermaker on Cherry River rolling copper
tubes for the flues in slow Shays used in logging one of the
last the photographer says to operate in that state crossing a
bridge two years ago Number 11 pulling stake cars loaded
with logs through the trees of early autumn

Digging a Hole in the Earth

On the first day of another year
I poke around the basement
among forgotten things—
grandmother's floral china,
dirt crusty flower pots,
a beached washing machine—
until I come to the rust-grown shovel
and lift it from the stand
of leafless lumber.

Perhaps unfrozen ground
is a sign from God knows whom
there is never too cold, nor too late.

Forgiven, at least, by the weather,
I take the shovel and begin to dig
downward through limp grasses
and the last of leaves,
carefully place the point of the blade,
the thrust of the leg,
the lift and shouldering aside—
I build a mound of soil and stone
the depth of any hole I dig.

But I measure only the shovelful.
Nor do I answer those who ask
what hole I dig,
what mound I build.

Flower garden
or grave,
who am I to say
the difference there is between them?

A hole through January
I tell them,
a mound for Orion to rise and fall from.

Firm But Sensible Eating
from The Boston Globe 6.13.94

Beware of these words:

>
> buttered
> creamed
> *au gratin*
> *béarnaise,*
> *au lait*
> crispy
> *à la mode*
> *au fromage*
> *beurre blanc*
> deep-fried
> *escalloped*
> *en croute*
> gravy
> *hollandaise*
> prime.

Try ordering fancy coffees instead.

Harlequin Off the Highway

Harlequin pulled off the highway.
For hours flashing headlights were telling him something
until at last, traveling more and more slowly, he realized what it was:
Harlequin was lost.

The map Pierrot gave him was wrong.

Harlequin was furious.
For years he had waited to be invited to the party
and it was just like Pierrot to go without him,
to mislead him,
to make the map indecipherable
by transforming the directions into a nursery rhyme.

Well, wherever it was, it was just like Pierrot.

Pierrot asked Harlequin to attend the party,
but now he would never arrive,
at night, in the fog, alone,
without any idea how he got here,
never mind there,
wherever there was.

Well, this was not strictly true.
He recalled a few turns that weren't on the map at all,
a few shortcuts that took him several states out of his way,
a few years mislaid here and there sightseeing,
so that actually he was about ten years late
and a few hundred miles away
from wherever it was he was supposed to be,
or not supposed to be,
for Harlequin knew he was not supposed to be here,
wherever here was supposed to be.

Harlequin searched the car for another map,
perhaps one left by Old Harlequin,
who had driven the car to work for years.

He found one at last in the trunk,
water damaged and torn
from years of lying beneath the spare.

Carefully, Harlequin unfolded the faded blue and green paper
into the familiar, broken-hearted shape of Ohio.

Harlequin left that state years ago,
and it was too late to go back,
wasn't it?
With only half a tank of gas
and no prospects for a job?

Oh, why didn't I become a stockbroker,
live in Akron,
and grow zucchinis?
Harlequin asked the moon
perched like Pierrot in the arms of Columbine.

Harlequin knows somewhere there's laughter,
and Pierrot discoursing on the sex lives of arthropods to Columbine,
who sips each word like sherry.

Pierrot knows everything but the color of rain,
which is neither here nor there
for Harlequin,
sitting in his car, lost
in the singing of spring peepers.

Blue Jay Feather

When the sea died and vanished under the earth,
I emptied my pockets of everything:
all the insects, birds, flowers, trees, horses, fish, stones, moons,
even the night itself.

Afterwards I was unable to touch a single word.
My feet felt so light I did nothing
but watch trees sway against the clouds.

And so I walked in silence,
with nothing in my hands
until I came upon a blue jay feather
that spoke to me saying,
I am the tongue that fell from your mouth
when you lost the names of everything.

I picked up the feather,
that serrated edge of the sea.

Broken Glass

Shattering glass.
We heard that, all right.
I was already sitting up in bed
when my wife asked,
What was that?
Did you hear it?
By then I was heading toward the living room,
thinking maybe the glass doors
on the wood stove burst.
The stove was still warm,
the doors intact.
Sounded like broken glass.
That was the first either of us
said anything about glass.
But nothing was broken.
No shards scattered over the dark floor
like some upside down planetarium.
Not in the kitchen,
living room or basement.
Check the door.
I did. Locked.
We went back to bed,
but I couldn't sleep.
I thought of the time
I was in high school.
A few months after my grandmother died,
I snuck into her house with a girl I was seeing.
We were on the sofa
when a cut-crystal pendant
fell from a lamp.
Out of the blue.
I took the girl home.
I saw her once after that,
my grandmother I mean,
but I don't believe in ghosts or
angels, so I hope whatever

broke that glass wasn't one of them
marking the house for illness or death.
Whatever fell last night
didn't leave any fragments
to piece back together.
In the morning, I saw a crow
glide from the roof,
a black speck into another blue,
but the bird
was a different matter.

Falmouth, Early Morning

It's always 3:10.
The walls float on the bottom of the ocean.
Shadows spiral up.
I'm holding my breath.
Outside, tree spirits dance
in falling ashes of light—
the moon sets fire to the sun,
consuming the oxygen.

Bronze butterflies,
cowbells, golden stones, and chicken hawks
all look for home.

Then I remember his tongue
growing like a purple eggplant
no one could pick from the vine

and I know I am not alone.
You are somewhere nearby.
I listen to your breath breaking on a far beach,
long, low lines
hissing with white air
I swim toward,
kicking my legs like a dolphin's tail,
pushing for shore
until my knees
cold as seawater
come aground
in the hollows
behind your knees.

Forsythia and Lilac

I thought we'd killed them,
forsythia and lilac dug from the earth,
roots severed with the shovel blade,
then replanted in this barren sand
dumped when the glacier grew tired
and lay down its burden of stones.

Arguing over where to put them,
we mixed a slurry of peat, soil, and manure,
cut them to the ground and soaked the roots,
then buried them to bind their wounds.

Nothing slept all winter.
Now they unfurl new leaves over a new land
they claim as their own.

Do they dream at night of lost roots?
Do the stumps ache when it rains?
Do they grope under the earth for the past?

They don't know why.
They just pick up and go on,
willing to give spring a chance.

Concord Afternoon

Better there are clouds today.
Better than sun!
Blue-veined white marble.
Some things too distant to touch.

If ever I knew
I have forgotten by now why we chose
to spend the day walking the dry paths of history
where everything is veiled by dust,
made invisible by water,
those essential qualities of life.

Perhaps there is no more than this:
that together we cross the old river,
sunk to its roots,
and emerge on the far side:
friends who find by afternoon a common field
to silently take root in.

I choose these lilies
all sword-shaped leaves and funneled flowers
drawn for a day from green shadows by an irresistible heat and light,
you the purple loosestrife stalking the sun
far to the west, over Ohio.

Another Poem About Stones

1
I walk an old path.
Ghosts of dragons brush the leaves
along wet branches.

2
Trees vanish ahead.
I cannot say why I grieve
for old, stolen stones.

3
Along the path,
white arbutus flowers trail.
The ground lies uneasy.

4
In a single step
I disturb the sleep of quail.
Below us, the sea.

5
Two stones lay
among wild blueberry bushes.
Stone hunters left them.

6
A small red pine grows
from a crease in the granite.
I rest in the shadow.

7
Almost I hear them,
the stones carried to the sea.
Wave breaking on wave.

Leaf, Moon, Word

A leaf whispers with the slightest wind.

Not even the deepest root knows which leaf
will trace the moon, as I will never know
which word reaches you,
a soft hand breathing in darkness,
touching what is invisible.

Just as only one of many hands
will sweep a glance from your face,
so only one of my words will ever grow
as a leaf on a blue limb
branching across a white moon.

Perhaps the word doesn't even exist,
having yet to evolve from silence
as the moon evolves from absence.

Perhaps I haven't spoken the word,
for some words are ghosts
searching their way back from the dead
through the mouths of the living.

Or perhaps the word has already
fallen from the branch of my tongue,
burrowed into your skin
and taken root in your earth,
speaking with your voice
just when you believe you have nothing to say.

Bird House

What was left lay in the grass
beneath the bluebird house,
too scattered to name
but likely a nuthatch.

A pair moved in a month ago.
We didn't mind.
Everybody needs a home.
We saw her peer through the box hole
as he flew back and forth to the feeder
or walked upside down.

So when I saw nothing of them,
I took the step-stool
and peered into the dark.
Listened.
Tapped the side of the house.
Nothing answered.
Nor swooped from the sky.

I pulled the wire pin
and swiveled the floor.
The house was packed full.
With a screwdriver I scraped
bits of bark, wood and leaves,
feather and what looked like hair.
Dirt blew into my eyes.

The nest slid to the ground.
No dead chicks,
just four eggs smooth as jelly beans
white crimson speckled
as with a mother's dried blood.
Two broke with the fall.
I set the nest in a chair turned
with its back to the wind.

That's when I saw a nuthatch
jump from the feeder:
first to the lattice wall,
then the railing,
the table,
the arm of the chair,
cock its head and stare,
fly back to the feeder,
eat a few seeds,
then swerve for the bird house
and pass, into the woods.

On a Photograph of Walt Whitman

Who are you, Walt Whitman?
Sitting there, slouch-shouldered,
hands in pockets,
full-bearded
beneath your wide-brimmed hat.

You said I would find you under my boot soles.
Said you'd be up ahead, waiting, looking back.
Who knew you'd be in my bedroom?

From behind the glass wall
separating your world from mine,
your gaze finds me no matter where I sit —
slow, heavy, patient —
considering just what kind of fool I am.

The sea has run away tonight,

leaving the bed of stones it sleeps on,
fleeing into the darkness of planets.

Sea, where have you run to?

I hear your long white breaths
collapse with exhaustion
but cannot find you beneath any star.

Have you run away with the moon again?

Tonight the moon unfolds like a magnolia blossom.
I walk with my moon shadow along the shore
washed clean as glass when the sea left
sharing the soles of my feet,
a long-winged blackbird, skimming over the sand.

When I call,
the sea doesn't answer.
The wings of my shadow never waver.

The Man Who Fell in Love with the Moon

Once a man fell in love with the moon.
It happened slowly,
the moon only a sliver of light
growing slowly until one night
blossoming into a white dogwood tree.
The man lay down on a bed of darkness
and let the moon fill his arms.

Then, without a sound,
the moon began to dismember itself,
cutting off a foot, an ear,
a hand, a thigh,
until nothing remained but a shadow.

The shadow was powerful,
causing all the rivers of the man's body
to swim towards it,
crossing back and forth twice each day.

And slowly the moon reassembled itself,
reattaching a breast, a knee,
a lip, a hip, a hand
until the moon stood full before the man.
But this time the moon
dropped leaves into the man's arms.

The man wanted to flee
the bed of darkness but his arms
were full of leaves.
Besides, there was no place
where the moon couldn't see him,
or any way to stop the fish
rising to the surface of his veins.

Tree Time

I sought a metaphor in the trees,
something that would say how in Ohio
oak, ash and maple drove me behind the mower
I wielded like an angry bee its stinger,
from their girth I hid behind playing kick-the-can,
from the black legs I ran among chasing fireflies at dusk.

They force me to say I no longer live among them
but in some other place near the sea
where trees don't grow so tall
and a cat hauled off the road next to the mailbox
lies clench-mouthed, grieving its lost life.

I had no idea a body can unravel so fast,
that in a week or so
all that's left is a filthy black and white rag
laid upon the earth for the sky to kneel upon.

Leaving This

When you are still —
breathing as trees do
where spiders weave funnels of mist in the grass,
and the yellow shafted flicker raises its red head —

you leave this for another place
sustained by whispers
you understand no more
than does a leaf the tree.

The Story of Falling

All winter I've thought of leaves
and their solitary journeys
from summer's airy laughter
to the silence gathering along the stone wall,
how from the moment
of detachment from the limb
each leaf is defined —

much as the boy who falls
from the sun falls
from the shadow of wings, falls
from his father's cries
collecting among the waves.

Starling in a Cedar Tree

A starling climbs the cedar limbs,
stops here and there to listen,
cocks his beak then flails the bark and eats
whatever squirms or crawls:
the starling knows what to listen for.

A starling steps the wooden stairs
of a monument green with age
for grub or beetle, moth or caterpillar,
alert to the sweep of wing or leg:
the starling knows what a tree is for.

A starling leaps, iridescent, brown-black wings
rowing rung by rung to the sun.
His shadow blinks, then flutters down
and blinks again before he leaps once more:
the starling knows what the rowing's for.

ODE TO THE CATBIRD
for Eric Edwards, July 22

Why do you mew at dusk?

Shakespeare enters Shylock at the Stationer's
as Shelley signs the register at a cheap Mont Blanc hotel
and lists, in Greek, his occupations:
Democrat, Philanthropist, Atheist.
Destination: *L'Enfer*.

But the day grows less heroic:
Benét born in Bethlehem
neither beast nor savior,
Sandburg dead in Flat Rock,
unenthusiastic,
89-years-old forever.

Burns dies yesterday when
Crane enters Ohio's promised land
and Hemingway barbecues a palm
fêting himself in Málaga with fireworks;
Thoreau goes to jail tomorrow for a dollar,
but these aren't the days we haunt.

You mew.

Flaubert works in a post office
until seized by epilepsy into fiction,
but the woman on the naked bed
pares her toenails,
oblivious to his small desires —
dead letters delivered on a sandy rural route
with boxes too far from the road
and other birds silent as noon.

Oh, deliver us from Teaticket
and endless vicissitudes of summer traffic.

You mew.

Clouds walk empty-handed into the sea.
On the horseshoe crab's last day
he becomes his poetry.

When shall we, too, be born
weeping with words?

Leda and the Swan

The swan's bite.
For Michelangelo, at least, this is no rape,
no rape, at least, of woman:
    the left arm hangs over the back of the couch
    to anchor against the swan's thrusts,
        open-handed, unclenched;
the right hand curves gently, resting on the strong thigh,
    articulating what cannot be spoken;
        the raised left leg hooks between her
    lover's folded wings,
the right beneath presses him to the mysterious flower
    open beneath
        his webbed feet.
    He flies through
    forever,
        clasping her mouth in his beak.

    For Michelangelo,
the act in time is timeless:
    the swan lies beyond his lover's hands,
        unafraid
of history or woman:
    carefully combed hair,
        heavy-lidded eyes,
    soft soles of her feet
ravish the god with her body's power,
time and history engendered by love's timelessness:
    mother of twins,
        mother of twins.

    The swan's kiss:
one cannot fear the gods and goddesses, he knew,
        and live.
Delicately, tenderly, the long-necked, beak-headed swan
    snake-reaches toward the proffered face,
taking pear-breasted, muscular Leda's lower lip
        in his bill.

On the Infidelity of Birds

Birds, long regarded as paragons of sexual fidelity in the animal world, are being cast in a much less virtuous light as a result of a flurry of studies of our feathered friends.
The Boston Globe

        Even the birds
             are not faithful.
After centuries as
        role models of monogamy,
              scientists have learned the birds
                  fool around.

        Female black-
            capped chickadees
invariably seek
        males with higher status than their mates.
            Male mallards sexually force
                themselves on

        unwilling
            female mallards.
Among indigo
        buntings, one third of nestlings are not
            sired by the nest mate. Female
                bluebirds

        leave their own
            territories
searching for other
        sex partners. No wonder mute swans paired
            for life seldom speak to one
                another.

                You have to
                            wonder, one asks,
        does monogamy
                    ever exist? Despite wings, birds leave
                            genetic tracks, records like
                                    sexual

                library
                            cards. Yet they can
        be discreet, flying
                    to the next neighborhood of trees. Birds'
                            ability to fly
                                    gives them

        huge opportunities. They,
                        too, risk parasites,
                venereal disease, and other
                            non-sexually transmitted
                                    diseases.

                These ills make
                            no difference
        whatsoever. None.
                    Benefits, for them, outweigh the risks.
                            A mixed reproductive
                                    strategy,

                it turns out,
                            is best for birds.
        To produce the most
                    offspring, male birds, like huge insects, should
                            mate indiscriminately.
                                    Female birds,

                    rather than
                            put all their eggs
        in one basket, so
                    so to speak, should seek better males. This way
                            some should survive if their nest

                              partners prove
                  sterile or
                        weak. Some surmise
            that male trespassers
                  who hold off nest mates and over-
                        power females display
                              better genes.

                  Whomever
                        the father,
            females place all eggs
                  in one nest. It's perfectly logical,
                        assuming her mate's territory
                              is adequate.

                  Cuckolded
                        barn swallows
            may reduce the care
                  given to young, but philandering
                        females know repercussions will be
                              few since male

                  barn swallows
                        fear losing those
            chicks they have sired. How
                  these birds are able to determine
                        which eggs have been fertilized
                              by them

                  and which eggs
                        are fertilized
            by other male barn
                  swallows, research scientists have yet,
                        like the meaning of baseball,
                              to discover.

At Forty-four

On the day my age
turns twice the day I was born on,
I wake to the staccato hiss of water sprinklers
tracing circles on my neighbors' lawns.

Fragment on Tree and Leaf

The tree is not unkind
when it chokes at the stem the leaf
that sang and danced all summer.

Returning to a Place

I. November

I take the small shovel,
a galvanized pail,
and poke among dead stems,
scraping away wet oak leaves
and the cracked black skulls of pignuts,
searching for daffodils
bought ten years ago,
planted by my mother,
and left behind.

II. January

My shadow slips over
the stone wall
and disappears among the trees.

III. April

Between the mower and rakes
in the bottom of a two-gallon pail,
nests of dry roots
curled like hair around the bulb's end —
a few green shoots
pierce the air.

Arguing with Bakhtin in the Employment and Training Office in Wareham, Mass.

I don't know who starts this.
But here I am.
Sitting at a table with a young mother and her father in a black
    leather jacket,
a fat folder of papers documenting the kids are hers,
both of us filling in claim forms with blunt pencils
while trying to remember anything from the last eighteen months
when Bakhtin walks in, yammering about the pathetic attempt of
    the state
to aestheticize the event with aqua carpeting and matching cubicle
    dividers,
fluorescent lighting masked by egg carton grills
when anyone can see we're in a cheap strip mall
on Route 6 where the stores have gone to hell
since they connected I 495 to the Buzzards Bay Bridge.

He is quite content with the absence of poetry.
The prosaic, he says, is the only way to experience
the historicity of unemployment,
the lack of either chaos or order
that allow becoming,
the freedom that brings you to this place,
the multiple potentialities leading at every instant in all directions.

I tell him I don't see much beyond the two o'clock orientation.
I tell him I don't remember when I got here or see when I'll get home.
Time, he says, is irreversible;
only if it is unrepeatable and unpredictable can one be truly free.

Who's free? I ask.

What do you think I am?
An apostle of freedom, for god's sake?
Without constraints
nothing is real,
not even the lack of reality.

I don't understand.

Of course you don't. How can you understand yourself
without stepping outside of yourself?
You can't even see yourself without a mirror.
There is no possibility of meaning from inside.

I'm done filling in the form,
so I hand it in and step out into a January drizzle.
Bakhtin follows.
I tell him I'm not sure if collecting unemployment is ethical.

Ethics? If ethics were an object of knowledge,
then philosophy would provide a moral education.
But ethics is not a matter of knowledge but wisdom.
And wisdom, my balding friend, is not systemizable.
Life is not finalizable unless you're dead.

I tell him I just want to pay some bills within my own lifetime.

Don't you see! he screams.
The only way to construct models of openness
is to locate unfinalizability in ordinary processes
such as filling out an unemployment form with a dull pencil
among all the young mothers because they
are and have been the product of accumulated tiny alterations
constituting the daily effect of being!

Cars drive by in the rain.
I pull out the keys to the Corolla.

Being outside creates the possibility of dialogue
that reveals meanings that are unknown,
that are not realized
within the self
but exist as potential!
I tell him I've got to go, that I hate to end our conversation,
but we'll talk again some day.

You idiot!
Haven't you heard a word I've said?
He opens the door and slides into the backseat of my car.
If you stop talking now, you'll never exist.

Hands

They come empty
of all but a few sleepless hours
clicking their tongues,
empty of all but dry rivers wandering
their flexible earth
in search of an ocean to drown in.

As the leaves possess light,
they are transformed by what possesses them,
possessing what they never possess,
becoming what they possess.

A Drunken Moth

I found a moth swimming in my glass of wine,
trailing ashes from wet wings,
so I fished it out to see if it would live
and after a few moments the moth flailed,
then tipped over on its back, drunk,
staring at the heaven it had fallen from.
I thought the insect must be dead,
but only fish fall belly up, said Gide,
and, having caught its breath, the moth swam the backstroke on
    my hand,
so I got the creature back on several legs again,
hoping it would take off like a struck match for the empyrean,
but it twirled mad as a maple seed,
a small stone skipping in the grass at my feet,
worshipping the god it knows.

The Fish in the Bays Grow Fatter

The fish in the bays grow fatter
and the grass dries blonde.
The sun rises and travels
like anyone with somewhere to go
while cicadas claque
and children are born.

No one stops,
can stop,
anymore than a traveler
leaving a village
can be sure
or care
such a place existed,
that he drank a beer and
talked about the local team
and watched the sea.

Only the body disbelieves
such a thing
and grows quietly in far places,
unaware a war ended
and its allegiance changed,
goes on with the daily business at hand,
goes on with the same small preparations
for whatever is to come

as the fish in the bays grow fatter
and the grass dries blonde,
the sun rises and travels
like anyone with somewhere to go
while cicadas claque
and children are born.

STONE, SHELL, CRAB

They are burdensome
as gifts are burdensome:
stone, sea-bitten shell, and crab's lost life
carried home to guide us,
who wish only to be young,
into growing old.

Only then can we return
them to the life taken from them
when they cried from the sand,
Speak to us,
and we will tell you secrets.

Who Knows

There is little solace sitting beneath
the near full moon bleached as a fish
out of water, nursing wounds.

Why do we say these things?
Pride?
The lack of human dignity in a world

where violence is more valuable than words?
Poetry, said the old man,
isn't made of grievances but griefs.

So We Sit

So we sit,
the old grey cat and me,
traffic left in the front yard.

Nothing disturbs us behind the house.
Even the ants leave us lonely
as rails rusting the sleepers
beyond the stone wall.

With each gust hickory petals
tug from their branches.
The dogwood lifts arms of blossoms.
The cat sleeps.

A titmouse shrieks to the feeder,
daring me to scare it away.

Sleep

As I go to sleep each night
ghosts of women I loved
leap from the shadows lying on the floor

and lie down and curl on my bed like cats.
They hum softly,
lying close to me,
circled among my legs all night
yet eluding my face in darkness.

Under their presence I roll from side to side
and am prevented from doing so.
Dreaming, I ask one to marry me,
to come back to the bed she left years ago,

rising for a drink of water
and never returning.
Having died from my world into their own

they reappear
with quiet smiles and voices.
Once they would lie down and curl

on my bed like cats.
Now their forgiveness
wakes me before daylight.

The Body of Rain

I stayed home
and left a light on.
The body of rain fell

welting the street,
tracking the grass.
Before going to sleep

I opened the door
and called once.
I didn't expect that folded rag

to get up from the road
and waltz in.
We'd thrown that away.

No, I thought a cat's soul
might come home
one night

before going wherever
a cat's soul goes.
The body believes

in nothing,
trampling the grass
like rain.

Low Windows
for Frank

Three times the minister (if we call him
that now) falls upon the mystery of death
though nothing seems mysterious about the closed
coffin of another suicide, 41, lived with his mother,
sold books then worked in a home for disabled
men and volunteered in this new church, if we call
it that, white walls and upper windows shuttered,
white vinyl mini-blinds, though not the lower ones.

Beyond, yellow March grass, trees, and black-ribboned
utility poles carry incomprehensible conversation,
may he find peace, while rain falls in the hereafter.

At the Boston Ballet

The dancers are beautiful,
their bodies lithe as seaweed
and powerful as handguns,
hard, compact, ready to fire,
the play of the musicians beautiful,
the sets, lighting and costumes beautiful,
and I'm happy, sitting in the loge above the stage,
that there's a place for dance
that there are those who so love the movement
of the human body, life's energy born
long before the military-industrial complex
and terrorists began reducing civilization to rubble,
house by house, bridge by bridge, market by market,
school by school, hospital by hospital,
saving us from each other.

Cobalt Blue Rock

I awaken.
The moon on her knees washes the floor,
water swirling white across her swollen feet.
I need a rock.
Not just any garden variety rock.
Lots of those lay about
doing nothing all day,
not even answering the phone
or getting the mail from the box.
No, I need a blue rock.
Lime green or scarlet might do in a pinch,
but blue as the earth will be best.
No one can accuse such a rock of remaining silent.
No one can say she hasn't heard such a blue rock.
I will be king of the universe!
I look behind the dresser,
under the books on the nightstand,
beneath clothes piled in the corner.
In short, everywhere.
And nowhere.
The moon moves on, washing the wall.
No blue rock.
I have no desire to search between the waves of the sea.
The moon sighs, climbs out a window.
I should write a note reminding
myself to look inside my shoe
where a small puddle remains
but instead fall asleep.

What's at Hand

I spot the hawk through a gap
in the crenellated top of a worn-down
stone wall edging along Old Dock Road,
the rabbit's shoulder pinned to the green lawn
by the hawk's yellow claw with leg
feathers wind-flared like jodhpurs beneath
the full belly mottled and common,
the tail red as a stiff-bristled brush,
black-banded with tips dipped in white paint,
the hooked beak bloody.

The hawk,
a few feet away,
turns and stares.

The cotton-tail's head lolls to one side,
the eye a black period ending a sentence,
a flopped ear above the chest ripped
open, bones bared and stringy guts
strewn causing three girls strolling up
from the beach to say *that's disgusting*
on the way to their summer house.

Inarticulate Hands

The first time I loved her
my hands were so thirsty they drank
the water from the cells of her skin
and she flew off like a leaf on the autumn wind.

The second time I loved her she appeared
at a distance, years later, and my hands
hid in my pockets, silent and fearful,
sentenced to a life of washing dishes and scrubbing floors
if they harmed her with their tongues,
yet leaving her uncovered as snow fell through tree limbs.

If I love her a third time
these hands must learn to speak softly,
through the vowels and consonants of their fingertips,
the language of spring rain feeding the cold ground.

Living by Words Alone

I want to live by words alone.
I want them to be the coffee I wake to,
the water I work with my hands,
the wine I count leaves by.

I want to live by words alone,
to be nourished by their sounds,
to take from them all the proteins,
all the fat and carbohydrates my body requires,
all the minerals and vitamins,
all the leaves, fruits, and vegetables,
sugars and starches
necessary to feed the cells of my body.

I want to live by words alone,
to lie down at night with them,
to feel their small teeth biting my shoulder,
to feel their thighs between mine,
their fingernails along my arm,
to taste their breath of cigarettes and oranges,
to explore them on the tip of my tongue.

Poem Without Words

This is a poem without beginning, middle or end.
How voices touch one another,
hold each other in their arms of vowels and consonants,
then turn and walk away
like waves toward the sea —
that is some other poem.

For these words are not poetry
but the last stars in the night sky
I took down when all else faded into light
and held in my bare hands —
hands that could never hold another pencil.

Then I knew these words
will never be a poem
with a beginning, middle or end,
taken up by my red roots
like calcium into my bones.

So when I perform the simplest action —
raise the cup to my mouth,
wash in the shower,
sweep the floor —
I write another line
in the poem without words.

Tableau Vivant

On the night road I glimpse at the far edge
grazed by the car's headlights a grey shadow:
a squatting coyote taking it to the street
in the other lane. The head turns
trailing my slow approach, unconcerned,
as if asking, *What're you going to do about it?*

Having passed by I flash my lights at an oncoming
car whose driver will think there's a cop ahead
however unlikely in these woods and not, as I hope,
watch for a ghost oblivious to everything
but the body's urge wherever it arises and there
isn't anything I, or you, can do about it.

Coyote Visit

When my wife yells to look quick
the coyote runs back up the abandoned path
into the woods but soon returns.
The color of trees, large, watching us
up by the house, it crosses the backyard
behind the Buddha meditating
and up another path to the compost pile,
noses grapefruit rinds and onion skins
then retreats through the brush
on a trail we hear more than see.

Then the screech begins.
Not a rabbit squeal. Owl?

Fox.

Over the screeching a crow flies in circles
restless
raising a ruckus.

The screech repeats like slow heartbeats.

The crow lands and circles and lands
restless, raising a ruckus.

My wife picks up a birch stick and starts
up the overgrown path.

Stops.

The crow flies off.

November Night

Orion is up tonight.
Seeing a friend, I think of the years
light spends traveling.

On the Poems of Frederico Garcia Lorca

My pockets are empty
as the soles of my shoes.

My hands search everywhere,
wandering through dry valleys of cotton
in search of marigolds
flowering in November light,
gold coins spent celebrating
life on earth.

They found the sound of my eyes
the sound of my tongue
the sound of my ears
the sound of my nose
the sound of my fingers.
Such senseless things.

So I bring these words
left beneath a tree
by a man on his way
to a firing squad.

Cemetery

He is crouched,
making his unspoken way around the grave,
back bent as a toadstool
the dried root in his hand
smashing the clumped brown earth
until the mound lies smooth as a blanket
on the unsettled bed.

Looking down,
I see the hands at rest with one another,
head tilted on the pillow,
the dark-filled glasses
she insisted on wearing those long days
looking up
through the blued air
to the ever falling
light hidden stars
falling now.

Shaken by a Dream

in which I couldn't remember
the name of the aunt who sold refrigerators at Sears,

I toast some bread and butter it
remembering how when she made pies,
mom would roll out the excess dough
sprinkle sugar and cinnamon,
then roll it up
cut slices and bake them into sweet crusts.

The aunt was Frieda.

Snake Crossing

On August 16th, ten days after the snake vanished into the earth,
Anthony Ferrari confessed that Tut, a venomous,
banded Egyptian cobra, bought mail-order for fifty dollars,
had eluded his captor and returned to the underworld
after sunbathing on Ferrari's front lawn in Stoneham, Massachusetts,
across from an elementary school whose students
created a sign: Snake Crossing.

Older residents weren't amused to learn
Tut can live all winter without eating,
only to reappear in spring when everyone,
distracted by daffodils and cyclamens,
overlooks the ground opening at their feet
and Death bursts forth to claim his bride.

Ferrari, whose real name, he confessed, is Barry Corbett,
works as a male model and once smuggled Tut into a nightclub to impress
    a dancer.
One bozo, a herpetologist complained to *The Globe*, *gives us all a bad name.*

I, too, confess the other day
when I stepped from the basement door
barefoot, book in hand,
air whistled in my mouth —
that reaction associated by Freud
with the first separation from the mother in birth —
before I recognized the *narrow fellow in the grass*
and also felt zero at the bone,
how Lawrence saw the poisonous snake at his water trough to be a god,
how with a shovel I could sever the snake in two
when the snakes of childhood emerged from their underworld,
the ones I feared in dreams,
the one my father shot the head off, poking from the woodpile,
the black one by Crystal Lake we thought might be a water moccasin
that my father, sister, and I stoned to death.

In November, a student found Tut curled on a shelf, next to his lunch.

The Dog

How the future wends its way into the past
or the past into the future
or which crime he's sent from Ireland
to avenge is not said.

But this time I spot him
from my second floor window
in a house like the one in Ohio.
I know he carries a gun
from the way his shadow
leans across the yard.

There's no escape now.
My only chance is to take him by surprise.
What the hell.
If I'm going to die
what does breaking my legs matter?
(As an infant I leapt from my crib
breaking my collarbone,
so I know what I'm doing.)

I hide at the top of the stairs.
When he's half way up,
I spin around the corner and jump,
taking him with me before he fires a shot.
At the bottom of the stairs I kick in his head.

He bleeds surprisingly little.
But if he's found too quickly
I'll never escape,
so I stuff him like Polonius in a closet
and decide that next time,
I'll take the dog.

Virgin Mary Reported in Market
The Boston Globe, May 19, 1998

Pilgrims
>continued trekking
>>to a New Jersey
>supermarket yesterday,

upon word
>that an image
>>of the Virgin Mary
>had appeared

on a freezer
>door.

>>The image,
>said to be a silhouette

of a woman
>in a hooded
>>garment,
>first appeared

Thursday
>and lasted through
>>the weekend,
>witnesses said.

They said
>the vision had
>>appeared
>inside the thick,

double-paned
>glass door
>>of a freezer
>containing sausages,

burritos and plantains
>>at a La Conga Supermarket
>>>in Jersey City,
>>a largely Hispanic and

heavily Catholic

                    working-class
                              city a few
                    miles west
of New York.

          Although the image
                    had faded away
          by yesterday,
people kept
          arriving
                    at the store.

          Hundreds of visitors
left candles,
          handwritten
                    messages and
          flowers,
said Jarmina Cortes,
          owner of a flower
shop next door
          to the supermarket,
                    who sent
          her six children
to leave a bouquet
          of a dozen
                    white
          roses
at the freezer.

          The people are
                    still coming.
          Many are sick
and tortured,
          she said.
                    They are
          looking
for help.

                    Asked about
                              the image,
                    Michael Hurley,
     a spokesman
                    for the Roman Catholic
                              Archdiocese
                    in Newark said:
I am led to believe
          that it is certainly
                    not an apparition.
          But could I
swear that it
          wasn't?
                    No.

Vow

Not in the presence of God
but before these friends,
before these moths and winter trees
watching like ghosts rooted in air
and beyond them the sea
crossed by all-witnessing winds
and vanishing stars
(unless friends, moths, trees, sea, winds and stars
be the presence of God),

not with divine assistance
but with my tongue,
eyes and hands,
my heart and lungs,
and beyond them my blood
born in the hollow of my bones
and electrons dancing
along the pathways of nerves
(unless my body's assistance be divine

and our lives be the lives of some god),
I vow to love you faithfully
as long as we both shall live.

Confession

I confess
to the god who doesn't exist
I confess
like one who suffers a blow to the head
I confess
I have lost my native tongue
and speak through translation
word by word
line by line
I confess
I confess
I no longer understand
the air I breathe
I confess
from beginning to end
unmoved and
worse
bored so that I rise from the chair
and open the cupboards
searching for something to eat
and select nothing
I confess
though I comprehend each
syllable and synecdoche
symbol and metaphor
I confess
even the crow
who belongs to my writing group
now turns its back to me
as if one of us
doesn't exist
before slipping
no more than a shadow
among the trees.

The Journey of the Hero at the End of the Twentieth Century or: Ted Meets Sylvia in Hell

Gilgamesh. Odysseus. Aeneas. Dante. Ted.
Half way through the course on Great Books,
there stands Ted Hughes,
poking through winter like a stick through snow,
answering the call to adventure,
entering the earth's darkness
on his journey to the underworld.
Only this time there is no crucifixion,
no Get Out of Hell Free card,
no companion twin to fight,
no witch goddess to sleep with,
no sibyl to thread the leaf-clogged lanes,
no old man to foresee the way home.
Ted's too late for the tea party:
no need to pack a golden bough,
Charon never balks at ferrying the dead.
No need to throw honey and meal,
Cerberus won't bark if you haven't got a heart.
Not that Ted has lost everything.
When Minos winds his tail nine times,
Ted turns into a crow whose oily wings
float him down, down, down
past East Limbo, Lust, and Lower Gluttony,
past Avarice, Upper Prodigality, and Anger,
across the River Styx and beyond West Heresy
before entering the walled City of Dis.
Only this time there is no sacred marriage.
No father atonement, no apotheosis.
No elixir theft.
No flight from the kingdom of dread.
No resurrection.
No ruby slippers.
No light-saber.
No invisibility cloak.
He doesn't even reach the bottom of the story.

Which isn't to say there is no boon that restores the world.
For having crossed the river of boiling blood,
Ted enters the Wood of the Suicides
where he breaks off a twig of Sylvia
with red leaves. She cries,
Why do you break me?
Why do you tear me?
Is there no pity left in any soul?
Beware, beware!
This time she charges nothing for her words,
nothing to touch her clothes, her flesh, her bone,
all scorched like a Thomas's held twenty-five years in a toaster oven,
black wings stirring the ashes.
Sylvia becomes inspired:
she snatches the crow
and, just as she said she could,
eats it.

Like air.

Dream of the Ghost Without Hunger

Having been granted night passage across the sea without name
I step onto land, the sea moving in darkness,
a traveler walking down a hillside beneath a whorl of stars and planets,
the ground covered by wet stones I slip on,
a vampire fearful of greeting my shadow.
So I turn and retrace my fallen steps
across the past I have stumbled through,
walking uphill until I come to a house
I enter without knocking.

Around a long table, people dressed in white are celebrating.
She sits at the center, talking, laughing.
There are no empty chairs.
Yet no one notices my presence—
the candles do not flinch from the breath
of a ghost without hunger from his journey,
so relieved am I to find her
safe, secure, happy
that I ask for nothing,
not even a glass of water
or a glance from her hands.

I had said angels do not exist.
And that night I dreamed of after our deaths—
far from whatever remains of us
dancing amid the vibrations of atoms—
searching for each other.

Ode to the Crossword Puzzle

Nights, when I roll back and forth
like a jellyfish pushed and pulled by tides,
I wake to find a woman lying next to me.
The woman is not my wife.

And though I have loved her
and will love her
we do not make love.

Rarely, when she feels very affectionate,
she sings softly in my ear
strange stories filled with vivid images
I repeat over and over,
hoping to memorize them by morning.

Otherwise, we work shoulder to shoulder
on the Sunday crossword puzzle.
She whispers the clues across and down,
and when I cannot solve their mysteries
she sifts the sands of my memory
and corrects my bad spelling.

Slowly I slip beneath waves of sleep,
her voice dark as the sea
until only a shadow speaks.

My wife sleeps.
Vowels wash away with the stars.
The evidence falls to the floor,
the pencil warm from her hand.

Elixir

I, too, am sorry
that I bring you not
that glass of water
that relieves all thirst
and heals all wounds
but a glass of tears
bitter as the sea.

Poem for the New Millennium

These hands of ours.
Dutiful, obedient, carrying out their morning commands
like servants who seldom complain:
carry this orange, lift that cup, hold this knife,
yet silent, isolated, slouching against a hip
or withdrawn into their lonely lint-filled rooms.

Perhaps we should teach them a few words
such as worn travelers to foreign countries learn
to navigate a strange, light-filled world
or to recite poems they love: ripe peaches,
tall grasses, warm bread, light oil, cold water, white carnations.

Then as we walk along a forest path
they might emerge from the holes in our sleeves
and speak with each other before flying off through the trees.

Crow(s)

1. Crow Attack

Black feathered planes swoop
low strafing with machine guns.
Leaves kick and fall to the ground.

2. Japanese Crow

Crow bows to drink from its mouth.
Summer passes overhead.

3. Crow Reflection

Two shadows meet.
One throws back a shot of water.
One staggers.

4. When Crows Plagiarizing Badly Move Next Door

Silence flees and hides beneath a crown of bees.

5. Dysfunctional Crows

Crows talk too much. And too
loudly. All afternoon, like old people
unable to hear, shifting from tree to tree,
unsatisfied with the branch they grasp,
their arguments running unresolved
long after I'm dead.

6. Crow Haiku in Way Too Many Syllables

A crow disguised as a Ford F150 pickup
glides down Main Street.
Cars scatter like small birds.

7. Postmodern Crows

Crows caw nothing evermore.
They do not symbolize death.
Or the resurrection.
Or the new moon at midnight.
Or a lover's eyes.
Or Buddha.
Or Satan.
Or Moby Dick.

8. Crow Shadows Revisited

No longer tied to our feet
crows are useless for poetry
and are addressed only by lesser poets.
Free of hypertextual feathers
crows answer to crows,
kick up a ruckus in the trees for the hell of it,
tear the wings from smaller birds,
splash in the birdbath,
play leap crow in the trees
with nothing to answer to.

On the bright side,
walking is easier without being
dragged into the trees.

9. Near Crow Haiku with the Syllables in the Wrong Places

Distant thunder.
Green fish school with one mind.
No crow in sight.

10. Not a Crow Haiku, or Even a Tanka

Crow carries a cherry tomato from the compost
to the birdbath to wash away dried coffee grounds.

11. The More Crows Change

In the town forest
crow gangs defending their cribs
screech crow obscenities.
Montagues and Capulets.
Sharks and Jets.
Bloods and Crips.
All wear identical
iridescent colors.

12.
A Flock of Crows (generic crow haiku)

black black black black black,
black black black black black black black:
black black black black black.

Jim Morgan grew up in Silver Lake, Ohio. After attending Case Western Reserve University, he received an MA in Creative Writing from Boston University and an MA and Ph.D. in English Literature from Tufts University. Retired as a professor in the humanities department at Massachusetts Maritime Academy, he lives with his wife in Falmouth, Massachusetts. His previous books of poetry are *Harlequin's Guitar: A Fable in 67 Improvisations* and *Procession of Souls*.

www.ingramcontent.com/pod-product-compliance
Lightning Source LLC
Chambersburg PA
CBHW060414080526
44583CB00012B/564